HELEN AS AN
ADOLESCENT
WITH HER DOG

HELEN AND HER BELOVED TEACHER, ANNIE

HELEN READING A BRAILLE BOOK

...LEN WITH PHIZ, 1902

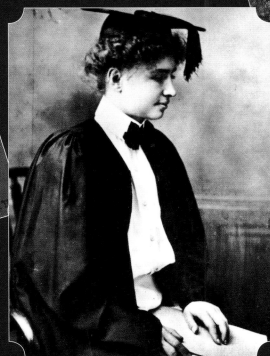
HELEN AS A RADCLIFFE GRADUATE, 1904

HELEN BY THE WATER

AUTHOR'S NOTE

"It is a rare privilege to watch the birth, growth, and first feeble struggles of a living mind; and moreover, it is given me to rouse and guide this bright intelligence." —ANNIE SULLIVAN

"At the beginning I was only a little mass of possibilities. It was my teacher who unfolded and developed them." —HELEN KELLER

This story is about two extraordinary women: Anne Sullivan Macy and Helen Keller. Their remarkable relationship began in 1887 and lasted until Annie's death in 1936.

Annie Sullivan was born in Massachusetts on April 14, 1866. As a child, she contracted a painful eye disease called trachoma, which left her blind in later life. Her mother died when she was eight, and just before Annie's tenth birthday, she and her little brother, Jimmy, who had a tubercular hip, were sent to a poorhouse. Not long after, Jimmy died. Annie lived in the poorhouse until she was fourteen, when she was sent to study at the Perkins Institution for the Blind in Boston.

Teaching Helen was Annie's first job after graduation. Helen became the core of Annie's life. Annie stayed with her pupil and friend until her death. In 1905, Annie wed John Macy, but the couple grew apart and eventually separated. Anne Sullivan Macy died on October 20, 1936.

Helen Keller was born on June 27, 1880, in Alabama. An illness in February 1882 left her deaf and blind. With Annie as her teacher, Helen made remarkable progress and grew to be an independent thinker and writer. She entered Radcliffe College in 1900 and published her autobiography, *The Story of My Life,* in 1903. With Annie's help, Helen graduated with honors in 1904, becoming the first deaf and blind person in the United States to earn a bachelor of arts.

Helen began working on behalf of the American Federation for the Blind in 1924. A lifelong advocate for people with disabilities, she traveled to many countries, wrote books and articles, and corresponded with writers, scientists, and world leaders. Helen was named one of the 100 most influential people of the twentieth century by *Time* magazine. She died on June 1, 1968.

Annie and Helen

BY DEBORAH HOPKINSON
ILLUSTRATED BY RAUL COLÓN

schwartz & wade books · new york

A NOTE ON ANNIE'S LETTERS

When Annie Sullivan arrived in Tuscumbia, Alabama, to begin teaching Helen Keller, she wrote letters about her experiences to Mrs. Sophia C. Hopkins, her friend and former teacher at the Perkins Institution for the Blind, back home in Boston. Annie had lived at Perkins from the time she was fourteen until her recent graduation, six years later. The letters begin three days after twenty-year-old Annie enters the Keller home.

MARCH 6, 1887

My first question was, "Where is Helen?" . . . I had scarcely put my foot on the steps, when she rushed toward me. . . . She is never still a moment. She is here, there, and everywhere. Her hands are in everything; but nothing holds her attention for long. Dear child, her restless spirit gropes in the dark.

Helen was not quite seven
when Annie Sullivan came into her life.
Annie had journeyed more than a thousand miles
by train to begin her first job, teaching little Helen.

Helen had been a healthy baby,

but at nineteen months a sudden illness

left her blind and deaf.

She had learned to shake and nod her head,

pull her father's hand when she needed him,

and pretend to butter bread when she was hungry.

But Helen could not communicate with words.

So when she didn't get her way,

or people didn't understand what she wanted,

she flew into angry tantrums,

lashing out at Martha, the cook's little girl;

her loyal old dog, Belle;

even Nancy, her favorite doll.

Helen was like a small, wild bird,

throwing herself against the bars of

a dark and silent cage.

Annie knew how Helen must feel.

Ever since Annie was a girl, she'd had a painful eye disease,

and she had been partly blind until an operation helped her see.

Annie also knew that it was Helen's anger and frustration

that kept her from learning.

MARCH 11, 1887

She has tyrannized over everybody. . . . To get her to do the simplest thing, such as combing her hair or washing her hands or buttoning her boots, it was necessary to use force.

Each day with Helen brought a new battle.

If she cried—which she did often—

her family always gave in.

Not Annie.

When Helen put her hand into Annie's ink bottle

while she was writing letters,

Annie gave her some beads to string instead.

Once, at breakfast, when Helen stuck her hands
into everyone else's plates to grab food,
Annie refused to let Helen touch hers.
She asked Helen's family to leave,
then locked the door and prepared for battle.

Helen pinched! She hit!
She threw herself to the floor and kicked.
Annie would not give in.
It took two hours, but in the end
Helen ate her own food with a spoon
and folded her napkin when she was done.

Annie asked Helen's parents to let her move with Helen into a cottage close by.
Separated from her mother and father for just a few weeks,
Helen became calmer
and accepted Annie's rules and teaching.

But Annie still had to help her find a way
to express her needs, her thoughts, her feelings.
Helen needed *language*.

How could Annie teach her?
After all, Helen could not hear words or see the motions
of the two-handed sign language many deaf people use.
So, from her very first day with Helen,
Annie had been trying another way—
the manual finger alphabet she had learned at Perkins,
which uses special hand positions for each letter.

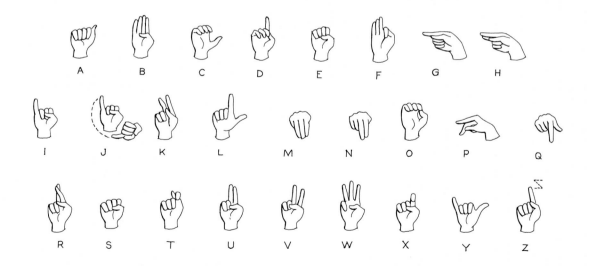

With one hand, Annie finger-spelled into Helen's palm,
hoping she would learn words by *feeling* them.

It worked like this:

Annie might place a doll in Helen's lap so that she could touch it.

Then she would move her fingers against Helen's open palm,

making the hand motions for each letter in turn: *d-o-l-l.*

Her skilled fingers would form a word—a pattern Helen could feel.

Annie would do this with familiar, simple objects,

m-u-g, m-i-l-k, or *c-a-k-e*—

all things Helen could touch or smell or taste.

But although Helen quickly learned to mimic these finger-words,

she didn't understand that each motion was a letter,

that letters made up words,

and that words could be names for things.

She didn't know that the cold, sweet taste on her tongue was called ice cream

and the soft petal brushing her cheek was a rose.

Helen still needed the key to language.

Annie spelled into Helen's palm all day long.

Like someone on a windy peak

trying to kindle a fire for warmth,

Annie kept hoping for a spark to catch.

Then, one day, Annie took Helen
outside to the pump.
As cool water splashed over Helen's hand,
Annie spelled *w-a-t-e-r* into her other palm.
Suddenly the rush of water
and the touch of Annie's fingers
flashed upon Helen's mind
like lightning in a midnight sky.

APRIL 5, 1887

The word coming so close upon the sensation of cold water rushing over her hand seemed to startle her. She dropped the mug and stood as one transfixed. A new light came into her face.

At once Helen sank and patted the earth.

G-r-o-u-n-d, spelled Annie into her hand.

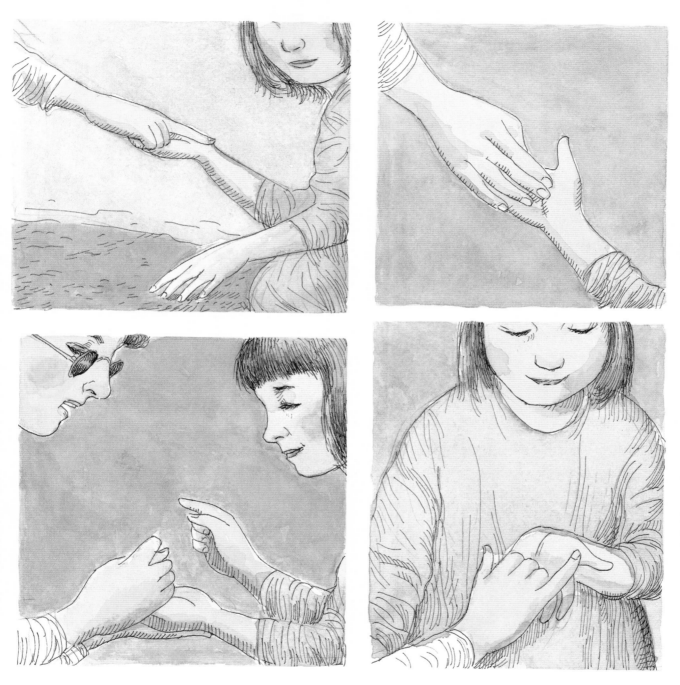

The nurse came by with Helen's little sister, Mildred.

Annie spelled *b-a-b-y* into Helen's hand.

Helen pointed at Annie.

T-e-a-c-h-e-r, spelled Annie.

Now Helen began to devour words,

minute by minute, hour by hour.

Annie realized that Helen was learning language just as a baby does.

Mothers and fathers don't give babies vocabulary lessons

or worry about teaching grammar—they just talk.

All on her own, young Annie invented a brilliant new way to teach:

she would talk into Helen's hand

the way people talk into a baby's ears!

So Annie "spoke" to Helen constantly and naturally,

spelling rich, wonderful sentences into her palm.

Annie made the world their classroom.

Get your hat and we will go out for a walk, she might spell.

And even though Helen had learned only the words *hat* and *walk,*

she grasped what Annie meant.

MAY 8, 1887

Helen is learning adjectives and adverbs as easily as she learned nouns. . . . She noticed that one of the puppies was much smaller than the others, and she spelled "small," . . . and I said "very small." She evidently understood that very *was the name of the new thing that had come into her head; for all the way back to the house she used the word* very *correctly. One stone was "small," another was "very small."*

Helen loved the gentle fluttering of a butterfly in her hand,

the moist, soft feel of moss,

the sweet-scented meadow breeze against her cheek.

She crowed with delight to touch a litter of squirming puppies.

When Helen petted one, Annie spelled *p-u-p-p-y* into her other palm.

Then, drawing Helen's hand over all of them, she spelled *p-u-p-p-i-e-s.*

Helen held up a finger for each puppy she touched.

F-i-v-e, spelled Annie, teaching her the number.

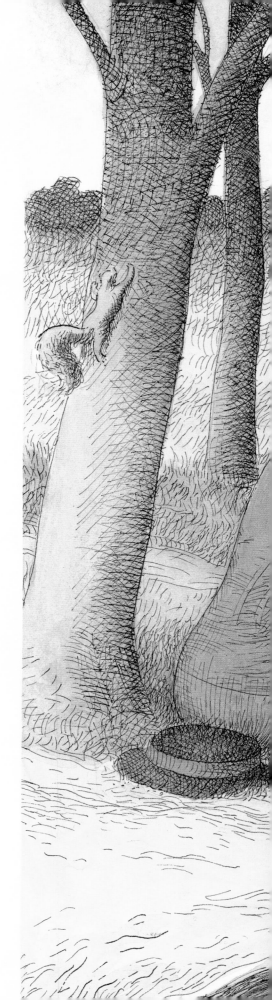

MAY 16, 1887

The weather is fine, and the air is full of the scent of strawberries. . . . I feel as if I had never seen anything until now. . . . Near the landing there is a beautiful little spring, which Helen calls "squirrel-cup," because I told her the squirrels came there to drink.

Each day when they walked to the river,
Helen bubbled with questions about
all that she touched, tasted, and smelled.
Why do flies bite,
and could they learn to stop?
Who put chickens in eggs?
And when she felt a wriggling piglet,
Helen wanted to know, "Did the baby pig
grow in an egg too?"

To help Helen understand sounds,
Annie put frogs and crickets into her hands,
so that she could feel them vibrate and move
as they croaked or chirped.

Once, Annie gave her an egg to hold
just as the tiny chick inside was pecking out.
Helen could feel the newborn chick's body
vibrating as it peeped—
"Chip, chip!"

Sometimes Annie thought Helen "listened" with her feet.
By sensing the vibrations in the floor,
she could recognize her mother's footsteps,
or the *thump, thump* of baby Mildred crawling.

To teach words we use all the time,
Annie put Helen's dress *in* a trunk, and then *on* it.

She let Helen feel a *hard* ball, then a *soft* one.

Together they wound a skein of yarn,
quickly and more slowly,
while Annie spelled *wind fast!* and *wind slow!*

Annie even found ways to teach Helen about things
she could not touch or smell.
Once, when Helen paused, frowning,
after Annie had asked her a difficult question,
Annie touched Helen on her forehead.
Then she spelled *t-h-i-n-k*.

Soon Helen had learned hundreds of words

and could count to thirty.

When she was thirsty she could spell

Give Helen drink water.

One day, when Annie asked Helen to bring her some water,

the little girl tried this excuse, finger-spelling,

Legs very tired. Legs cry much.

She was happier now, and hardly ever lost her temper.

But one day, Helen asked, *What do my eyes do?*

Annie explained that while she herself could see things with her eyes,

Helen saw them with her fingers.

After a moment, Helen spelled, *My eyes are bad,*

then changed that to *My eyes are sick.*

JUNE 19, 1887

During our walks she keeps up a continual spelling, and delights to accompany it with actions such as skipping, hopping, jumping, running, walking fast, walking slow, and the like. . . . She knows four hundred words besides numerous proper nouns. In one lesson I taught her these words: bedstead, mattress, sheet, blanket, comforter, spread, pillow. *The next day I found that she remembered all but* spread.

Soon Annie set about teaching Helen to read.

First, she showed Helen how finger-spelled letters

stood for the letters in the written alphabet.

Using a special book with raised letters,

Annie put Helen's finger on an *A*,

while finger-spelling *A* into Helen's palm.

Helen learned quickly, understanding that the written alphabet

was just another way to make the same letters she could finger-spell.

Putting letters together to form words came next.

Annie placed Helen's finger on the raised letters for the word *cat*,

finger-spelling it into Helen's other hand.

Again, Helen caught on right away.

Soon she would sit with her book,

searching with her fingers for words she knew.

Annie and Helen's mother cut up sheets of words with raised letters

so that Helen could practice making her own simple sentences.

Annie also taught Helen braille—a code that uses dots
to stand for letters and words,
which makes reading with the fingertips much quicker.
In time, and with practice, Helen would learn to read
whole books in braille, printed for the blind.
And with a special braille typewriter that printed the raised dots,
Helen could write—and even read her own words.

Helen often went with Annie to the post office,

and wanted to write letters like the ones

Annie mailed to her friend back in Boston.

Since most sighted people couldn't read braille,

Annie showed Helen how to write block alphabet letters

using a special grooved writing board placed under a sheet of paper.

Helen wrote with her right hand

and guided the end of her pencil with her left forefinger.

The grooved lines on the board helped her make her letters and words straight,

just the way lines printed on paper do.

That summer, Helen's father took her on a short trip,

and Annie went along too.

Helen learned the names of everyone they met.

She taught some children to finger-spell the alphabet,

and a little boy let her hold his rabbits,

trying to finger-spell all their names for her.

A girl showed her how to dance the polka,

and she even made friends with a fuzzy little poodle.

Helen missed her mother

and was bursting with things to tell her.

Now, for the first time in her life,

Helen had a way to share her heart.

And so, just like Annie,

Helen wrote a letter home.

Helen's first letter home:

Helen will write mother letter
papa did give helen medicine mildred will sit
in swing mildred did kiss Helen teacher did
give helen peach george is sick in bed
george arm is hurt anna did give Helen
lemonade dog did stand up.
conductor did punch ticket papa did give
Helen drink of water in can
carlotta did give helen flowers anna will
buy helen pretty new hat helen will hug
and kiss mother helen will come home
grandmother does love helen
good-by

For my daughter, Rebekah, and my nieces, Ellie and Kelly,
the wonderful teachers in our family;
and in honor of the many extraordinary teachers it has been
my privilege to meet in schools across the country.
Thank you for the miracles you perform every day.
—D.H.

For Ralph and Terry—men who face adversity—
and Vicki and Gail—the courageous women who face it with them
—R.C.

Acknowledgments

Special thanks to Jan Seymour-Ford, research librarian, Perkins School for the Blind, for her gracious review of the manuscript, and to Timothy Salls, manager of manuscript collections, New England Historic Genealogical Society, for the use of the early photograph of Annie and Helen with her doll. Thanks also to Anna Miller at the Perkins School for the Blind for her assistance with photographs.

Grateful acknowledgment is made to the American Foundation for the Blind Helen Keller Archives for permission to reprint excerpts from *The Story of My Life* by Helen Keller, copyright © by Helen Keller. All rights reserved. Reprinted by permission of the American Foundation for the Blind Helen Keller Archives.

For Further Reading

Dash, Joan. *The World at Her Fingertips: The Story of Helen Keller.* New York: Scholastic Press, 2001.

Delano, Marfé Ferguson. *Helen's Eyes: A Photobiography of Annie Sullivan, Helen Keller's Teacher.* Washington, D.C.: National Geographic, 2008.

Keller, Helen. *The Story of My Life.* Edited by Roger Shattuck with Dorothy Herrmann. New York: W. W. Norton & Company, 2003.

Lash, Joseph P. *Helen and Teacher: The Story of Helen Keller and Anne Sullivan Macy.* New York: Delacorte Press, 1980.

Lawlor, Laurie. *Helen Keller: Rebellious Spirit.* New York: Holiday House, 2001.

Learn More About Annie and Helen Online

Anne Sullivan Macy: Miracle Worker; American Foundation for the Blind—afb.org/annesullivan

Helen Keller Kids Museum Online; American Foundation for the Blind—afb.org/braillebug/hkmuseum.asp

Perkins School for the Blind—perkins.org/vision-loss/helen-keller

Text copyright © 2012 by Deborah Hopkinson • Illustrations copyright © 2012 by Raul Colón
Photograph of Helen Keller and Anne Sullivan in July 1888 courtesy of Thaxter Parks Spencer Collections, R. Stanton Avery Special Collections,
New England Historic Genealogical Society, Boston. All other photographs courtesy of Perkins School for the Blind, Watertown, Massachusetts.

All rights reserved. Published in the United States by Schwartz & Wade Books, an imprint of Random House Children's Books, a division of Random House, Inc., New York.
Schwartz & Wade Books and the colophon are trademarks of Random House, Inc. • Visit us on the Web! randomhouse.com/kids
Educators and librarians, for a variety of teaching tools, visit us at randomhouse.com/teachers

Library of Congress Cataloging-in-Publication Data
Hopkinson, Deborah. Annie and Helen / by Deborah Hopkinson ; illustrated by Raul Colón.—1st ed. p. cm.
ISBN 978-0-375-85706-5 (trade) — ISBN 978-0-375-95706-2 (glb) 1. Keller, Helen, 1880–1968—Juvenile literature.
2. Deafblind women—United States—Biography—Juvenile literature. 3. Sullivan, Annie, 1866–1936—Juvenile literature. I. Colón, Raul. II. Title.
HV1624.K4H67 2012 362.4'1092273—dc22 [B] 2010031443

The text of this book is set in Aldine. • The illustrations were rendered in watercolor. • Book design by Rachael Cole

MANUFACTURED IN CHINA • 10 9 8 7 6 5 4 3 2 1 • First Edition

HELEN KELLER AND
ANNE SULLIVAN,
JULY 1888

HELEN AS A YOUNG
GIRL READING,
CIRCA 1888

HELEN,
HER DOG PHIZ,
AND ANNIE
SITTING
IN A TREE

HELEN AND ANNIE
FINGER-SPELLING, 1888

HELEN WITH HER DOG JUMBO, CIRCA 1888

HELEN AND HER
LITTLE SISTER,
MILDRED